Wreath Magic

Wreath Magic

86 Magnificent Wreaths, Garlands & Swags to Make

Leslie Dierks

To Jurgen with love.

Special thanks to Ann and Everett Colby for the generous use of their Asheville bed and breakfast, the Colby House, and to Patti and John Hill for opening their hearts and home to our camera. Thanks also to The North Carolina Arboretum for providing the materials and facilities for staff and volunteers to make the wreaths on pages 32, 73, 108, and 116–117. And finally, thanks to Fireside Antiques and Interiors for their kind loan of a French country cradle.

Design: Kathleen Holmes
Photography: Evan Bracken
Production: Elaine Thompson, Kathleen Holmes

Library of Congress Cataloging-in-Publication Data
Dierks, Leslie.
    Wreath magic : 86 magnificent wreaths, garlands & swags to make / by Leslie Dierks.
       p.   cm.
    "A Sterling/Lark book."
    Includes index.
    ISBN 0-8069-0578-6
    1. Wreaths. I. Title
SB449.5.W74D53   1993
745.92--dc20   93-25678
                                  CIP

10 9 8 7 6 5 4 3 2 1

A Sterling/Lark Book

Published in 1994 by Sterling Publishing Co., Inc.
387 Park Avenue South, New York, NY 10016

Created and produced by Altamont Press, Inc.
50 College Street, Asheville, NC 28801

Copyright 1994, Altamont Press

Distributed in Canada by Sterling Publishing,
c/o Canadian Manda Group, P.O. Box 920, Station U,
   Toronto, Ontario M8Z 5P9
Distributed in the United Kingdom by Cassell PLC, Villiers
   House, 41/47 Strand, London WC2N 5JE, England
Distributed in Australia by Capricorn Link, Ltd., P.O. Box
   665, Lane Cove, NSW 2066

Printed in Hong Kong

ISBN 0-8069-0578-6

Contents

This simple but elegant wreath combines branches of Fraser fir with small boughs of white pine, all wired onto a circular metal frame. Branches of leucothoe—also known as dog hobble—provide leafy highlights, and glistening galax leaves add the finishing touch.

Introduction

Wreaths and garlands and swags once made only brief appearances in our lives, usually at Christmastime or during the fall harvest. Today they are hung year-round and in nearly every room of the house. They have become such an important decorative element that there are few magazines or mail-order catalogs that don't feature several beautiful examples to tempt your desires.

Their popularity really isn't a new development. Flowers and foliage woven together into wreaths or strung as garlands have long been used to ornament our lives. In ancient times they were often worn on the head or around the neck. Early Egyptians wore floral wreaths as collars, and stylish party-goers in ancient Greece wore fragrant garlands around their necks or colorful wreaths upon their heads (a sort of combined jewelry-perfume).

The ancients also took their wreaths and garlands quite seriously. Individual plants were thought to have important, even mystical, powers. Some were believed to be harmful, and others therapeutic. Assembled together into a wreath, they were used to ward off evil spirits or to heal the sick. The *lei*, a circular garland made of flowers and foliage, is now commonly presented as a gesture of hospitality to arriving and departing visitors to Hawaii. It was originally an important element in religious rituals.

Gradually, ancient beliefs about plants evolved into symbolic meanings. Rosemary, which was thought by the Romans to improve memory, came to signify remembrance in the language of flowers and herbs. Sending messages through careful combinations of plants reached its height during the Victorian era, when true feelings could not be discussed openly. Elaborate "discussions" took place under the cover of a floral exchange.

Modern wreaths, swags, and garlands are much more likely to be found adorning our homes than ourselves. And, with the possible exception of those we make for the holidays, we are more often concerned with aesthetics than with symbols. This is a very liberating notion: we can allow our senses free rein to dictate the materials we want to use. If a particular flower appeals, use it in abundance. There is no need to determine if it has an unfortunate, underlying meaning.

On the other hand, if the idea of creating a Victorian-style floral message sounds like fun, by all means do it. This book is all about enjoying yourself during the creative process. There are only a few tricks and techniques to learn, and there is an entire world full of delightful materials to which they can be applied.

As you meander through these pages, you'll find a broad range of styles, from classical formality to unconventional combinations. Try some of each. You can find your true voice only by experimenting, and you may discover a talent you didn't know existed. Remember, there is no such thing as a "bad" wreath or swag, only one that you don't like.

More importantly, don't judge your own work prematurely. By their nature, most of these projects look distinctly unimpressive in their initial stages. Only when you've filled the last gap should you step back and give it the once-over. Even then there are remedies. Let's say you've just finished your first garland, and it looks pretty bland. Don't despair. With some brightly colored berries or flowers applied with a glue gun, or a few twists of ribbon woven into it, you can transform the ordinary into the exquisite. In fact, once you've had a little practice, you may find that those impressive examples you've always admired in the slick catalogs and glamorous magazines don't hold a candle to your own.

Materials

Evergreens

Choosing the materials to make your swag, garland, or wreath is one of the most exciting steps in the process. There is literally an entire world open to you. Some of the most traditional, and underrated, are evergreens.

Unless you happen to be an avid gardener, the word "evergreen" usually conjures up an image of Christmas trees, or perhaps the perfectly sculpted, rounded shapes dotting your neighbor's lawn. Chances are, there are numerous evergreens all around you that you have never thought fit the category because they are not displayed in these traditional ways.

Evergreens include the many species of needled trees such as pine, spruce, fir, and hemlock. These are commonly seen during the holiday season and can often be found growing wild in nearby woodlands. When cut and brought into a warm house, many are redolent with a spicy fragrance that can fill an entire room.

However, there are many equally attractive—but less commonly used—evergreen trees and shrubs. For a fine, needlelike texture, choose juniper, cedar, or cypress. A totally different effect can be achieved with branches from broad-leafed evergreens such as magnolia, rhododendron, mountain laurel, azalea, holly, or boxwood. Cotoneaster is another excellent and seldom used material. It is an evergreen whose small oval foliage becomes a deep burgundy when the weather turns cold. In the spring, its branches are covered with small white flowers. These are replaced in the winter with an abundant crop of red berries.

Ground covers such as ivy, periwinkle, and pachysandra are also good candidates. Their vine structure makes them a more fluid material than the stiff branches of trees and shrubs. They are ideal for garlands and make fine accents for wreaths and swags.

Flowers & Herbs

Flowers and herbs have a long history in wreath and garland making. We have generally lost sight of any meaning inherent to specific plants or the curative powers of wearing them. Our present forms of communications are much more direct than the "flower language" of the Victorians, and modern medicine encourages the use of an aspirin for a headache, rather than a crown of myrtle or mint. Now we enjoy flowers mainly for their beauty and the pleasures they bring.

When it comes to long-lasting arrangements, there is nothing more attractive than dried flowers. They are widely available from florists, herb farms, and craft shops, although you may find it more fun to dry your own. Many plants can be successfully air dried, which requires no special equipment and only a few specific techniques.

Pick your flowers and herbs on a dry day, after any dew has evaporated but before the blossoms are wilted by the strong midday sun. Cut the stems as long as possible, and remove the lower leaves. Drying causes considerable shrinkage, so pick more than you think you will need.

When you have enough, fasten small clumps of the same plant together with a rubber band wrapped tightly around the base of the stems. Suspend your clusters upside down in a dry, well-ventilated location. Avoid placing them near windows; exposure to moist air may cause rotting, and sunlight can fade the blooms.

Don't expect your flowers to dry overnight. It generally takes several days before all of the moisture has evaporated. Test a stem by bending it; if it snaps, it is ready to use.

Nuts, Cones, Pods & More

In terms of materials, a leisurely afternoon outdoors can often be more productive than a trip to the craft supply store. That's because some of the best materials available don't have price tags attached.

Whenever you're out exploring in the woods, open your eyes to the creative possibilities displayed overhead and underfoot. Bend down to touch the furry softness of a bright green clump of moss, or to pick up a fallen tree branch covered with pale silvery lichens. Everywhere you look, you'll find pods and nut casings with interesting shapes and gentle colors. The debris of woodland creatures—abandoned nests, fallen eggs, even a few bones—are special finds, and these make unusual focal points for your compositions. Here is where you will also find vines of all sizes and configurations. These can be incorporated into your design and/or used as a supporting base for other materials.

Open, sunlit fields and marshlands provide an altogether different set of opportunities. A wealth of forms and textures can be found among the seed heads of wildflowers and shrubs—milkweed, poppies, and sumac are but a few examples. Sun-filled areas are also where you will find most berry-producing plants. Some of the most popular berries are holly, pyracantha, rose hips, and bittersweet.

As you find yourself becoming an enthusiastic scavenger of natural materials, don't forget the rules of common courtesy. The object of your desire may be growing on private property. If so, be sure to ask permission rather than calculating ways you can sneak away unnoticed with your treasures. Then when you do pick, don't take it all; leave enough of the plant for it to return next year. By all means, never dig up a wild plant. Many wildflowers have become endangered because they have been overcollected.

Fakes & Other Such Things

For nearly every growing thing that exists in nature, there is a manmade counterpart. Not too many years ago, artificial flowers, fruit, and foliage were as plastic in their appearance as in their composition. Visible seams, little structural detail, and phony colors all contributed to their undesirability.

In the interim, fakes have gone from garish to glorious. There now exist some examples so authentic in appearance that you literally have to touch them to distinguish the difference between artifice and reality. Foliage has progressed from thick, rubbery paddles to carefully lobed and veined reproductions of nature. Flowers, once a clumsy blotch of bright color, now have gossamer petals with natural gradations of tone.

Artificial materials offer several advantages: they're easy to manipulate (i.e., their stems won't break when you bend them into uncomfortable angles), they can be packed away and used year after year, and you can disassemble your creation and reuse the materials elsewhere. Given their longevity, you may be concerned

about keeping them clean. There is no need to worry; both plastic and silk materials respond well to a light feather duster. For those silks that are too delicate to touch, an aerosol spray cleaner is available.

In terms of size, shape, and color, fakes cover all the bases. You can choose full-sized fruits and flowers, or miniatures. If you would rather match your favorite bedspread than mimic nature, you can find any kind of blossom—real or imagined—in every color of the rainbow.

The next logical step beyond imaginative knock-offs is to look at articles from your everyday life. There is no cardinal rule that says all garlands, wreaths, and swags must be made of natural or nature-inspired materials. Consider items that have sentimental value, or those that reflect a favorite hobby. A collection that is enjoyed but not easily displayed or an assemblage of small gifts can make a distinctive wreath or garland. Alternatively, let your funny bone direct your choices, and arrive at something totally nonsensical, totally impractical, and totally hilarious.

Bases

A base is literally the skeleton that holds your project together and gives it shape. It provides the support for those delicate flowers, sprigs of greenery, and collections of nuts and cones. Depending on your design, a base plays a more or less prominent role.

A swag may need no base at all. Many consist solely of the materials being displayed. Long sprays of relatively stiff materials and simple bouquets fit into this category. Other swags are shaped into arches or other forms that require a sturdy support. These can be cut from wreath bases or built by hand from the component materials.

For a garland, all that is essential is a central "spine" made of wire or cord. The simplest ones thread the individual components directly onto this backbone. Those that alternate popcorn with cranberries to grace the Christmas tree are good examples of that variety. Another common type of garland attaches clusters of foliage or flowers to the base wire or string. As with the first example, the base is there strictly for support, not to be seen. A third approach is to flaunt the base. Make it pretty or interesting to look at, and include it into your composition. Using this method, you can build your garland onto a heavy ribbon, a braid, a collection of intertwined vines, or just about anything else you can imagine.

Wreaths have the most specific requirements: they all need a base of one sort or another. Thus it is not surprising that you will find a wide variety available commercially. Natural materials include vines, twigs, straw, pine needles, moss, and even woven wicker. Other common wreath bases are made from rigid plastic foam (e.g., Styrofoam) or metal wire in single or concentric rings.

For any project, which base to use is determined mainly by the decorative elements to be attached. Larger materials demand a larger base to look well proportioned. Heavier items must be secured not only so they won't fall off, but to keep the garland, swag, or wreath itself from sagging out of shape. You also need to take into consideration the quantity of materials available. Nothing looks more pitiful than a scanty garland or a sparse wreath. If you have only a limited supply of whatever you want to use, scale down your project, but make it lush.

How you plan to attach your materials is another consideration. Each kind of base favors some methods over others. If you prefer to work with picks, a vine, straw, or foam base will work well. For materials that are wired in place, a sturdy vine or heavy wire base is the better choice. Floral pins require a surface that gives, such as straw or foam; unless anchored with glue, they will simply fall out of a vine base. If your method of choice is the glue gun, your options are wide open.

Some added tips for choosing a base:

Do you want the base to show? If so, choose one that looks attractive in its own right. One that contrasts in color or texture with your decorative materials is usually a better choice.

Foam is manufactured in gray, green, and white, but you'll often find that the exact shape and size you want is available only in white. That's okay. You can prevent the bright white from shining through like a beacon by covering it with moss, crushed spices, or ribbon.

If you collect your own moss to cover your base, microwave it for a few minutes to kill any insects that may have nested there.

Straw is heavier and bulkier than foam, but it is more resilient. It can be easily reshaped if you want to remove something and replace it elsewhere. After having several picks inserted into it, a foam base can look more pitted than the surface of the moon.

Thick, older growth vines, especially grapevines, make the sturdiest bases; they can support considerable weight before bending out of shape. On the other hand, slender vines such as honeysuckle and wisteria create dainty, intricate-looking bases.

17

Wire

Whether it is used to attach cones and berries or to strengthen the fragile stem of a dried flower, wire is an indispensable tool. You can find plain steel wire in any hardware store, but for classier results, you should seek out floral wire at craft stores or discount marts. Floral wire is painted green to blend with natural materials, and it is available in straight lengths, on spools, or in coils.

All wire is sold by its gauge (thickness): the higher the number, the thinner—and more flexible—the wire. Thick wire is suitable for shaping a hanger or attaching a heavy piece of fruit. Finer wire is preferable for clustering small bouquets of flowers or pinching bits of lace.

If your desire is to incorporate single dried blossoms into your composition, you'll be wise to wire the stems first. Nothing can be more discouraging than the sight of several headless sticks standing in the midst of your creation. With a very delicate flower, lay a medium-gauge length of wire next to the stem, and wrap the two together with floral tape. Otherwise, wrap a fine wire a few times around the top of the stem, near the flower head, and spiral the wire down along the stem's full length. Again, cover the wired stem with floral tape. Bulky stems can be removed and replaced with a length of medium-gauge wire. From the underside of the blossom, insert a wire up through the center of the flower. Extend it far enough to make a tiny hook; then pull the wire back down until the hook securely catches the blossom.

To wire a modest-sized piece of fruit, insert two wires perpendicular to one another through the bottom sides of the fruit. Bend all four ends down, and twist them together for a couple of turns. Wire a single nut by first drilling a tiny hole in one end. Add a drop of hot glue, and insert the wire into the hole. Cones are easily wired by hooking a fine wire around the scales near the bottom of the cone. Pull the wire tight so that it is hidden within the scales. Then twist the shorter end firmly around the longer one.

Wiring an item in place is advantageous when you're not sure of its placement. Hot glue is a fairly permanent means of attachment, but you can change your mind as often as you please with wire.

Yarn & Cord

In a pinch, you can substitute yarn for wire to attach your materials. Some designers actually prefer it because it is more flexible than wire. With a vine base, brown yarn or jute cord is practically invisible when tied inconspicuously.

Floral Tape

Not noted for its adhesive strength, floral tape is nonetheless an essential tool for hiding wires, broken stems, and the like. It can be purchased in dark or light green and in brown. As you wrap the tape tightly around your stems, stretch it slightly, and the tape will adhere to itself.

Picks

Floral picks are slivers of wood three to six inches (7.5–15 cm) long, with a sharp point at one end and a thin, flexible wire attached at the other. Green is the most common color, but they are also available in brown and natural wood. When inserted into a straw or foam base, they provide secure anchors for clusters of flowers or foliage, loops of ribbon, or pieces of fruit.

To attach a small cluster of natural materials, break or cut the stems so that they are about half as long as the pick. Place the pick adjacent to the stems, with the wired end close to the flower heads or foliage. (The pointed end should extend well beyond the ends of the stems.) Make a couple of tight wraps with the wire around the stems; then angle the wire downward until you eventually wrap the wire around only the pick itself. If you plan to keep the finished project for a long time, a recommended final step is to wrap the stems and pick with floral tape. This arrangement not only has a neater appearance, it will also help keep the cluster in place despite the force of gravity.

You may find that the wire at the end of the pick is not long enough to wrap all the way around your desired item. When that happens, use a longer wire to wrap around your object, and secure the loose end onto the pick. Other materials can be "picked" by gluing them directly onto the top end of the pick or by impaling them onto it.

Tip:
For better adhesion in a base, always insert your picks at an angle. A dollop of hot glue is added insurance.

Pins

Similar in concept to old-timey hair pins, floral pins have a U-shaped profile with an "S" at the head end. Don't be confused, but these are also called "fern pins" or "greening pins." By any name, they are ideal for fastening moss onto a base. They can also be used to secure a wayward blossom or to attach a small cluster. Pins don't have much holding power, so don't expect them to contain heavy items or larger bundles. To maximize their strength, insert them at an angle to the base.

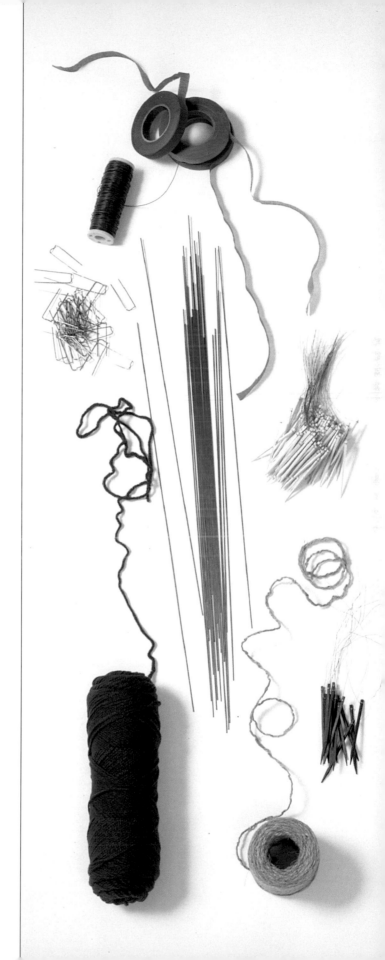

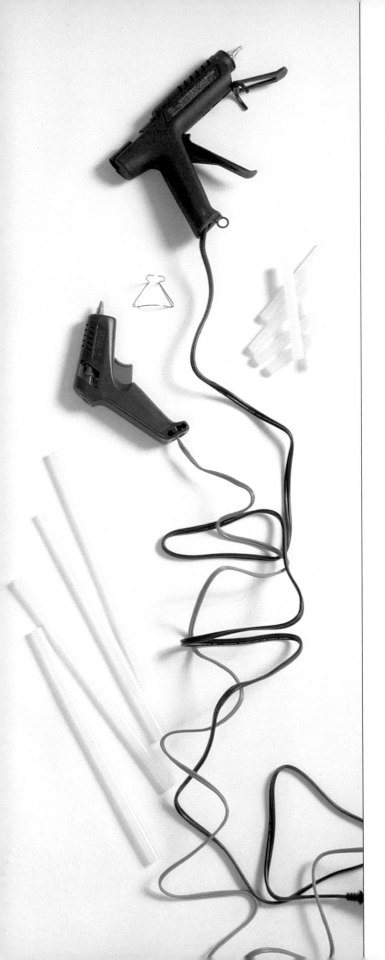

Glue Guns

For those who have never used one, buying a glue gun is an act of liberation. With a glue gun in hand, you will complete your projects so much faster and easier that you may be tempted to do twice as many!

Glue guns are similar in shape to electric drills, with pistol grips that make them easy to handle. They are available in all sizes and price ranges, and you can purchase them at craft shops, hardware stores, and discount centers.

Once you get the hang of it, you'll find that a glue gun produces a nearly invisible bond. The glue itself is sold in opaque rods that resemble candle wax. They range from a few inches (8–10 cm) to almost a foot (30 cm) in length and cost only pennies apiece. After it has been heated, the glue becomes nearly transparent when it sets.

No tool is simpler to use. Just insert a stick of glue into the hole above the handle, plug in the gun, and wait for it to come to temperature. Advance the glue into the heating chamber by squeezing the trigger. When you're ready, aim and fire a small glob of melted glue onto your object. Hold the glued item in place for several seconds to allow it to set thoroughly.

Hints:

Nearly all glue guns have one bad habit: they "drool" melted glue even when you're not squeezing the trigger. Protect your work surface with newspapers or an old tarp.

When plugged in, the tip of the gun gets quite hot and can be hazardous if allowed to come in contact with a flammable surface. Many glue guns are sold with a small, somewhat awkward wire stand. This serves to keep the tip of the hot gun off your work surface. If you don't like using it, be sure to substitute a piece of glass or a ceramic plate under your gun.

The glue extruded from the tip of the gun is equally hot. It can melt small holes in a foam base and cause burns on your fingers. You can rectify the problem with the base by covering it with moss, fabric, or other material. If you find that you're burning yourself too often for comfort, look for one of the warm-melt guns. They use glue sticks that melt at a lower temperature.

Gauge the amount of glue needed based on the size and weight of the item. To secure a flower blossom, a small dab is plenty. For larger objects, be generous with the glue and hold the item in place until it has set completely. Heavier articles should be secured with wire in addition to the glue.

As you work with the gun, you will notice an accumulation of fine, hairlike strands of glue on your project. They are easily removed as you go, or you can tidy up when you've finished.

Never leave a child unsupervised with a hot-glue gun. Even after it has been unplugged, a gun will remain hot for several minutes.

Making Bows

As with any art form, bow making looks effortless in the hands of an expert. For the novice, it can be pure chaos. That is why most card stores do a booming business in ready-made bows of all sizes and colors. Craft shops and florists also offer their services to make bows from the ribbons they sell.

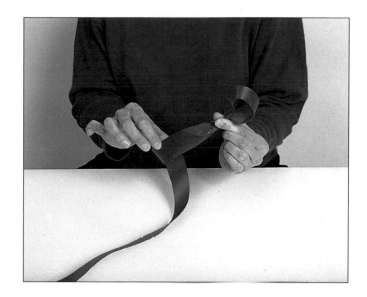

Why should you trust that lovely—and expensive—ribbon to your own hands? Because, believe it or not, you too can master the art. The whole secret of success boils down to three simple rules: pinch the center tightly, twist the ribbon so that the good side always shows, and anchor the loops securely with wire. Apart from these few guidelines, all you need is practice, practice, practice.

There are many equally successful methods for making a bow, but perhaps the easiest is to start at the front and finish at the back. Make your first loop and pinch it tightly between your thumb and index finger. If you are right-handed, hold the ribbon in your left. Now twist the bottom ribbon so that the right side faces up. Twist it tightly, right where your fingers have pinched the first loop. Then make a second loop opposite the first. Pinch it tightly together with the first loop. Add more pairs of loops, gradually increasing the size, pinching each in the center, and always turning the ribbon so that the good side faces up. Although you can shape the bow as you add loops, you may find it easier to stack the loops one under another, and shape them later.

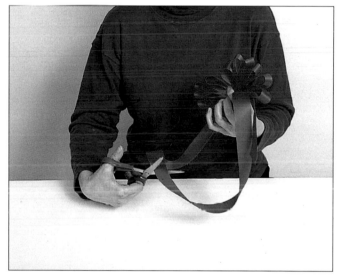

After you have finished making loops, the remainder of the ribbon can be used for streamers. Extend the ribbon as long as you want your streamers, double it back, and pinch it into the center of your loops. Cut the long loop with your scissors, making two streamers.

Now comes the trickiest part. Taking a 12-inch (30 cm) piece of 22-gauge wire (*not* 18- or 26-gauge), bend the wire into a tight "U." This looks like a small hairpin. Still holding the bow, slip the "U" straight down over the pinched center, squeezing the ribbon still more. Squeeze the wire at the back of the bow—needle-nose pliers are handy for doing this—and twist the wire a couple of turns. Your goal is to make the wire as tight as possible on the ribbon. To test for tightness, pull the wire in one direction, and the bow in the other. If it is tight enough, you will see no air space between the ribbon and the wire.

Congratulations! Now your bow is ready for its final shaping. Place your thumb on top, and move the loops wherever you want them. When you do so, the reason for wiring the ribbon so tightly will become apparent. Each loop is independent of the others; when you pull it into position, it won't unravel the rest of your bow.

One last word of advice: don't underestimate the amount of ribbon you'll need. A moderate-sized bow can easily consume four yards (3.5 m) of ribbon.

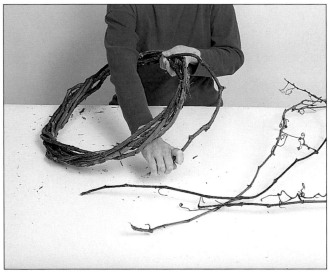

Building Wreaths from Vines

Exploring for vines is a pleasant first step to starting a wreath. You can use nearly any variety, and they're usually available at no cost. Spring and fall are the optimum collecting periods, when thick underbrush or a layer of snow does not obscure the runners creeping across the ground. The younger growth is easier to twist and turn, but you may want a few thicker sections for added strength. If the vine still has leaves attached, you can remove them easily by pulling the vine through your gloved hand.

Soaking the vines is recommended if they have sat for some time after cutting. This makes them more pliable and less likely to splinter or break. An interesting effect can be achieved by boiling the vines for about two hours and then stripping off the bark. After the boiled vines have cooled a bit, run them through your hand or between two pieces of cloth. The bark should peel off easily, leaving behind a smooth, waxy stem that looks like antique ivory.

When making any kind of wreath, you first need to decide the overall size you want. Be careful not to underestimate the size, keeping in mind that the thickness of the base materials and the size of the decorative materials will have a significant impact. If the base is too small, or the decorations too large, the central hole can close, diminishing the visual effect.

Begin your wreath by selecting two or three pieces of vine, each several feet (2–3 m) long. The overall length isn't critical; just stagger the thicker ends and wind the vines into a circle the size you want. With one hand, grasp the circle where the vines overlap, and, with your other hand, twist the longest vine ends around the bundle. Depending on the result desired, you can twist the ends in long, loose spirals or in short, tight revolutions.

Add more bulk or more spirals around the wreath by adding more vines. Tuck the heavier end into a new starting place, wind the vine around the wreath, and secure the loose end. For a classic design, make your spirals all in the same direction. Alternating directions produces a more casual effect.

Making Straw Wreaths

For a straw base, you can use any type of hay, alfalfa, or other dried grasses. You'll also need a spool of strong floral wire.

Start by taking a generous bundle of straw and squeezing it tightly in your hand, putting the thickest part in the center and tapering both ends. You can make the base as thin or as thick as you like, but a thickness of about 1-1/2 inches (4 cm) makes a solid wreath.

With your other hand, start to wind the floral wire around the bundle to hold it together. After securing the wire with a couple of quick, tight turns, pull the wire tightly around the straw in spirals about an inch (2.5 cm) apart.

Add new bundles of straw, keeping the thickness even, and start to curve the finished pieces into a circular form. Once you have the desired size, overlap the tapered ends, and wind wire all around the base in one continuous spiral.

If you're planning to use some rather weighty decorations for your wreath, you should build a wire-reinforced base. Take a coat hanger or other heavy wire, and shape it into a circle. Remember to make it large enough to accommodate the thickness of the sides. Then build the base as described above, but position the straw around the wire reinforcing ring. You can also use the ring as an attachment point for a hanger.

Adding Decorations to a Wreath

There are as many ways to decorate a wreath as there are designers. You can let serendipity be your guide, or you can follow a formula. The best advice is to experiment with different approaches to determine those you like best.

One classic approach to decorating a wreath is to apply your materials in a spiral. Starting in one spot, attach your first item or cluster. Angle it so that it is not sticking straight out of the base, nor lying flat against it. Your second item should be positioned to cover the means of attaching your first. Continue around the circle, adding materials at the

same angle and spacing. When you return to the starting point, lift the first item, and insert the last one.

Other designers like to divide the space into three or more sectors. This approach can help you achieve a wreath that is perfectly balanced in color and fullness. It is also a useful technique for designing an asymmetrical composition. By visually weighing the sectors, you can determine if your design is artful or merely lopsided.

A third method is to start by placing the largest, most significant decorations first. Then decorate the spaces around these with complementary shapes, colors, and textures. Finally, fill in any holes with the smallest of your materials.

Stringing Garlands

The Victorians, who raised Christmas decorating to an art form, were noted for the lush holiday garlands they laced through the railings of open stairways, draped over doors, or laid atop mantlepieces. In a more contemporary vein, the same concept can work in any room of the home and at any season of the year.

Evergreen garlands are certainly the most popular—they're readily available throughout the holiday season from Christmas tree vendors—but they only begin to tell the story. Garlands can be made of vines, dried flowers, ribbons, or any combination that strikes your fancy. Using floral tubes, you can also insert fresh flowers and greenery to liven up a dried arrangement.

Artificial flowers and fruits are among the most versatile materials you can use in a garland. In fact, many artificial flowers are sold in garland lengths rather than as single stems. These can be wired together and used as a base to which you can add other ingredients, both natural and artificial.

When you have occasion to buy a custom-made garland, you will pay a hefty price for it. The high cost doesn't come from the complexity of the garland's construction. It is deceptively easy to make. But, it does take time.

The secret to the structure of a garland is the single "backbone" that runs its full length. This spine must be strong enough not to break when the garland is suspended between two points. It must also be flexible enough to allow the garland to drape attractively across a piece of furniture or over a doorway. Heavy-gauge wire is commonly used as a spine, especially for evergreen garlands. Choose the gauge based on the weight of the materials you wish to display. A popular choice for dried flower garlands is jute cord.

Unlike decorating wreaths, where you can allow yourself total freedom in the order of placement, garlands have one very simple basic rule: start at one end and move toward the other. The reason for this is to allow each bundle of flowers, greenery, or other items to cover the means of attachment of the last. That rule aside, there are a few ways that you can attach your basic ingredients to create a garland.

For the beginner, it is probably easiest to make a number of small clusters of your base materials. Depending on the length and bulk of your materials, you will need as few as 20 to as many as 150 bundles to make a garland about six feet (1.8 m) long. (Now you know why the finished product is so costly!) Wire the stems of each clump together with a fine-gauge wire, leaving a tail of wire two to three inches (5–7.6 cm) long. Attach the first bundle by tightly wrapping the wire tail around the base wire or cord. Place each additional cluster so that its top covers the wire and stems of the previous one.

After you become more acquainted with the process, you may begin to feel that prewiring each bundle is an unnecessary step. In that case, simply position each cluster against the carrying line, and attach it directly in place with the fine-gauge wire.

You may also decide to dispense with the finer wire altogether. Some designers use the heavier base wire to wrap around each cluster and hold it in place. This is a more precarious technique than the other two. With this method, it is more difficult to achieve an even spacing between bunches, and the materials are more apt to slip out.

Hints:
Unless you intend to display your garland where it can be seen only from one perspective, you need to make sure it is equally attractive on all sides. As you construct it, rotate the garland frequently so that the bundles actually spiral up its length. This will prevent holes and flat spots.

Another way to assure symmetry is to construct your bundles *around* the central spine. This may sound like a job for three hands: one to hold the spine taut, another to position the materials, and a third to wrap the wire. To reduce it to a two-handed task, suspend your garland from an overhead beam or hook.

Creating Swags

Swags are generally easy to recognize, but their definition is not so straightforward. In years past, this was not a problem. Florists characterized swags as simple bouquets of flowers or foliage that were wired together and displayed upside-down. (Why it was determined that these arrangements should be made to dangle by their toes is still unknown.) This form of swag is still quite common, especially in the fall and at Christmas. Front doors across the nation sport handfuls of wheat or holly tied with colorful ribbons.

Today's swags push the bounds of creativity, making them more difficult to describe but much more interesting to view. Swags can form strong horizontal or vertical lines, gentle arches, or any number of other interesting configurations. In other words, swags are anything not long enough to be a garland, and not closed into a wreathlike circle or oval. Some especially interesting shapes can be created by making a base of intertwined branches and twigs.

Swags are ideal for anyone who hates to be constrained by rules. They can be sized and shaped to fit any location, and there are no standard construction techniques to remember. You can use whatever materials you prefer, applying them in any order or manner you like.

A few guidelines might be helpful. If you plan to use long stems of fairly stiff materials, you are likely not to need any type of base. Just wire the stems together, and they will be self-supporting. If you plan the addition of several smaller items in the center, wire and/or glue on a chunk of foam to hold them.

A sturdy support is necessary when you are building your entire swag from bits of moss or clusters of small flowers, fruits, or berries. To make a suitable base, use whatever you have at hand. You can saw a wreath base in half to construct an arch, or build a rounded, curving surface from lengths of vines or twigs. An antique tool, a raffia braid, or a handmade basket can be incorporated into your design to support the other elements in your swag.

Once you've made your first swag, you'll realize that there is nothing to it. Soon, there will be no holding back your imagination as you contemplate a tall, narrow wall in your bedroom, an empty space above the medicine cabinet, a "difficult" area over the fireplace....The possibilities are endless.

Choosing Your Design

With the images of lush and fragrant materials in your mind, as well as a strong desire to try some interesting techniques, you're probably ready to jump right in and start your first swag or wreath, right? Wrong. Before you begin your project, take some time to visualize how you want it to look when it is finished. Twenty or thirty minutes of advance planning can save you hours of taking pieces apart and rearranging them.

Imagine first where you want to display your handiwork. Certain spaces demand a swag, not a garland or a wreath. Decide how the location might impose other restrictions on materials or overall design. For example, if you are making an accent for your front door, you'll want to use materials rugged enough to stand up to the ins and outs of family traffic. You may also need to design something with a slender profile to fit between the front door and the storm door.

Apart from what and where, there are three other important design considerations. The first is scale. A massive stone fireplace would not be enhanced by a dinky wreath. Likewise, a bulky garland would not be appropriate for a dainty antique cupboard. In addition to overall size, take into account the mass of the individual materials. Full-sized poppies can be overwhelming if they are right in your face, and the intricacy of Queen Anne's lace is lost when viewed from across the room.

Your choice of colors should come next. Primary colors—red, yellow, and blue—make strong statements, but rich secondary colors such as purple and orange can also be intense. Keep in mind that yellow stands head and shoulders above other colors for conspicuousness. (That's why so many cereal boxes are yellow.) Colors also indicate moods: reds and oranges denote passion and warmth; blues and greens reflect cool serenity. Color theory aside, current fashion and your own decorating schemes will probably have the greatest impact on your decisions about color.

Last but not least, don't neglect texture. A wreath made solely of pine is rather plain. If you dress it up with some other greenery of varying textures, it becomes elegant. So elegant, in fact, that you may not want to add the slightest embellishment. (See the wreath on page 6 if you don't believe me.) Variations in texture create visual effects that are more subtle, but no less enticing, than those caused by combining colors. If you find yourself gazing appreciatively at your creation long after you think you should have grown tired of it, chances are its hidden appeal lies in its range of textures.

A spray of wild wineberry branches and a clutch of pine cones, pine branches, and tree fungi create the main focal point in this woodland wreath. In a harmony of color and texture, clumps of lichens and mosses are arranged around the balance of the wreath. All are attached with floral pins to a straw base.

Evergreens

*During the Middle Ages, it was common to bring boughs
of evergreens into the house to make swags and garlands
to brighten the cold and dreary winter months. This reaffir-
mation of life while nature is in the midst of hibernation is
every bit as comforting today as it was then. Because of our
strong tradition of decorating trees at Christmastime, we tend
to think of evergreens only in conjunction with the holidays.
Their versatility goes well beyond that few-week period, however. Alone, or in combination with other materials, evergreens
can look stylish and appealing any time of the year.*

Unconventional materials
arranged in the most traditional fashion can result in
a stunning wreath. Here the
"background" material con-
sists of two varieties of cypress
shrub, one a silvery blue and
the other a deep, forest green.
These are complemented by
sprigs of two broad-leafed
evergreens: andromeda *(Pieris)*
and holly. Soft, silvery
pussy willow grouped with
dark, spiky seed heads from
black-eyed Susans, golden
paulownia berries, and pale
pink heather create a harmony of colors and textures.
A branch of Siberian iris pods
completes the assortment.
The construction couldn't be
simpler; all of the materials
are picked into a straw base
in a spiral pattern. ∽

For an evergreen garland that does not shout "Merry Christmas" to all who enter, choose a broad-leafed shrub for your base and a bright yellow ribbon as your accent. This entry is bedecked with a garland made of rhododendron branches intermingled with ivy, a few stems of euonymous, and "roses" made from galax leaves. Because the rhododendron branches are so solid, you can do without a wire spine. Starting at one end, add branches one or two at a time, and wire them together with a continuous wrap of fine-gauge floral wire. The stem of the first branch is hidden by the leaves of the succeeding branches. Long ivy runners are allowed to wind lazily alongside and are attached periodically with wire. The euonymous and galax roses add some textural variety. When the garland has reached the length you desire, embellish it with a bright yellow ribbon threaded along its length, and add two large bows at key locations.

To make galax roses, you'll need about a dozen leaves for each. Start with a single, smaller leaf, and roll it tightly into a cone. Using floral tape, catch the bottom end of the leaf with the tape, and wrap the tape down onto the stem. Wrap a second leaf more loosely around the first, and secure it with tape. Add another and another, following the same procedure. After the fourth or fifth leaf, you needn't worry about catching the bottom of the leaf with the tape; just wrap the stems together. ∽

When you make your own garland, it takes almost no effort at all to build a matching swag. Here again a true base is unnecessary. The rhododendron branches are nearly strong enough to support themselves, and you need only to wire a small dowel (a tomato stake works well) across the back for stiffening. Point the branches outward from the center, together with some ivy and euonymous. Leave room in the center for a large bow and a galax rose. After threading the ribbon streamers through the greenery, add another "rose" at either end of the swag. ∽

Short branches of white pine intermingled with bunches of boxwood make a lush wreath, especially when mounted onto a thick straw base. Attach small clutches of each green onto picks, and arrange the clusters in a spiral pattern around the base. Using silver paint, spray a half-dozen magnolia pods and several branches of alder cones. Then pick them into appropriate locations around the wreath. Rather than making a conventional bow, form individual loops of silver metallic ribbon, wire them to picks, and attach each one deeply into the greenery for a contemporary look. ∽

If you're tired of the familiar pine and spruce, try using one of the broad-leafed evergreens for your base. This exotic-looking wreath starts with a foam ring that is completely covered with a spiral of magnolia leaves secured in place with floral pins. The asymmetrical floral drama results from two stems of dried protea, complete with their zigzag foliage, and a few sprays of yellow-flowering acacia. A tiny mound of dried moss adds eye appeal just above the flowers. ❧

Dried Herbs & Flowers

By their very nature, fresh flowers and herbs are ephemeral. Botanists call such plants herbaceous, which means they die back during cold winter weather. Mankind, never satisfied with such here-today-gone-tomorrow behavior, has devised a variety of methods to dry these plants so that they may be enjoyed all year long. Dried materials are the staples of floral designers because they are so reliable. If you're not already hooked, making a dried flower swag or garland will probably convince you that these materials have a magic all their own.

A sweetly feminine wreath results from a composition of silver, gold, and pink flowering herbs arranged on a plump straw base. Begin by making small bouquets of silver queen artemisia (including flowers and leaves), statice, goldenrod, larkspur, and pink globe amaranth. After wiring each bouquet to a pick, insert the picks into the base. Starting at one point, place the bouquets in a continuous spiral around the wreath. Be sure to cover the inside and outermost edges of the base so that the finished wreath is attractive to look at from all angles. Once complete, the only further adornment is a few nigella pods hot-glued in desired locations. ∽

When hung with a bright golden herbal wreath that is evocative of summer's glory, a favorite reading corner comes to life. This wreath is built upon an oval grapevine base, approximately 18 inches (46 cm) by 15 inches (38 cm). Its broad, mustard-yellow mounds of yarrow and bright orange Chinese lanterns sit amongst a textured sea of more delicate flowers: santolina, basil, goldenrod, catnip blooms, sweet Annie, and tansy. First, the background plants are clustered into small bundles and attached to the vine base, circling the wreath in a single direction. Then, after applying a bow at the base, several yarrow flower heads and Chinese lantern blooms are glued evenly around the wreath. ∽

Quick results can be had by starting simple. Wire two individual bundles of each of the following: eucalyptus, purple basil, and caspia. Grasp the two eucalyptus bundles with one facing left and the other right. Add the two bunches of purple basil, two or three poppy seed pods on each side, and the two bundles of caspia.

After tucking in a few stems of pink baby's breath and strawflowers, wire everything together in the center. Make a bow of burgundy paper ribbon together with mauve raffia, and wire it onto your swag. To complete the assembly, hot-glue four mini-bouquets of caspia around the bow, fanning out in each direction. ∞

Fifty Common Flowers, Herbs, and Other Plants Suitable for Drying

Amaranth
Anise hyssop
Artemisia
Baby's breath
Basil
Bay
Bee balm
Calendula
Carnation
Caspia
Catnip
Celosia
Chamomile
Coneflower
Dill
Dusty miller
Eucalyptus
Feverfew
Garlic
Goldenrod
Heather
Holly
Hydrangea
Ivy
Lady's-mantle
Larkspur
Lavender
Marigold
Mint
Nigella
Parsley
Pearly everlasting
Pitcher plant
Pussy willow
Queen Anne's lace
Rose
Rosemary
Safflower
Salvia (sage)
Santolina
Scented geranium
Statice
Strawflower
Sweet Annie
Tansy
Thyme
Ti tree
Wheat
Winged everlasting
Yarrow

Color, one of the most important elements of any composition, is a striking feature of this vibrant wreath. This wreath is also testimony to the fact that dried flowers can be every bit as distinctive as their fresh counterparts. Lady's-mantle covers about two-thirds of the grapevine base, leaving room to place a large bow after all of the flowers have been attached. Make small clusters of the lady's-mantle, and glue them to the base. Again using the glue gun, attach several branches of sumac berries at various points around the wreath. Follow with stems of lavender and everlastings in shades of bone, burgundy, and purple. Tie a luxurious bow of metallic ribbon, and glue it to the wreath so that its tendrils drape gracefully down either side. ↷

A rattan étagère gets a colorful lift from a lush garland of dried flowers. The mass of color and texture is achieved by wiring small but thick bouquets onto the spine. Shasta daisies combine with purple salvia, dusty miller, zinnias, and winged everlastings. Other bouquets include hydrangea, yarrow, marigolds, statice, and strawflowers. Bits of dried fern add touches of green. To unite the resilience of jute with the stiffness of wire, this garland employs a spine made from chenille stems connected end to end. Either jute or wire would be an appropriate substitute. ∾

39

Woodland Treasures

Nothing can put you more in touch with yourself, and the world around you, than an easy stroll through the woods. Before long, the worries of work and home slip aside, and you find yourself noticing exquisite details everywhere you look. Suddenly a moss-covered branch or an abandoned nest takes on a new significance. These are ideal forms and textures to include in your design. In fact, the process can become so captivating that you may want to devote your entire wreath, swag, or garland to the treasures you find.

Extraordinary results can be achieved with simple, found materials. Mosses, lichens, and several types of tree fungus combine with feathers from guinea hens, turkeys, chickens, geese, and peacocks. (Local farmers make good sources of poultry feathers.) Pussy willows are joined with large pine cones, the brown sheaths from philodendron plants, and seed heads from various wildflowers, including a local favorite called a devil's-claw. These and countless other "finds" are hot-glued onto a base made from heavy-gauge wire that is wrapped in hay and covered with Spanish moss. To build the composition, start at the top center with a large bow of upholstery ribbon and loops made from philodendron sheaths. (These are the brown outer coverings that are shed from philodendron stems when new leaves open) Thread matching ribbon streamers out from the bow toward the ends. Then add the larger pieces of moss, arranging them on both sides to balance the color. Fill in any holes with pieces of tree fungus, celosia, okra pods, palm inflorescence, and branches from a wild wineberry bush.

This swag looks so luxurious that you may be tempted to pick your neighboring forest clean of moss and lichens to replicate it. Instead, remember the golden rule of collecting—always leave enough of the plant to return next year—and adjust the size of your project accordingly. ☙

40

Vine bases are ideally suited to display a day's collection from the forest. Setting the stage are oak leaves, sweet Annie, and galax, all glued in an asymmetrical design around three-quarters of the base. At various locations around the wreath, tree fungus, which is glued into position, appears to grow out of the vines. Then bright ginkgo leaves and beech branches are tucked in as highlights. Finally, a tiny wasp's nest is glued to the exposed vine (on the upper right), and fronds of mountain sea oats are placed in the center.

From the feathery softness of miscanthus to the needle-sharp spikes of teasel, there is no shortage of texture in this exuberant swag. The base starts with a bundle of curly willow branches wired together in the center. Then a block of foam is glued and wired to the branches to provide a point of attachment for the grasses and pods. To prevent the foam from showing, it can be covered with sheet moss. Stems of miscanthus, eucalyptus, teasel, sycamore balls, leek flower heads, poppy pods, sea oats, and hydrangea establish the lines of the swag. Points of color are provided by preserved oak leaves, sumac seed heads, bittersweet berries, and bright yellow ginkgo leaves. In place of a bow, a wasp's nest acts as the central focal point. ❧

Shades of gray and brown predominate in this woodland arrangement. Create a suitable background with a straw base covered in Spanish moss. To make a natural "ribbon," wrap long philodendron sheaths around one side of the base. Bring two ends up and tie them into a decorative knot. On the other side of the wreath, concentrate several cones, sprays of pussy willow, and a few sumac and lotus pods. Fill in the bottom with tree fungus, several feathers, bits of lichen, and an abandoned bird's nest. ∽

On occasion, it pays to follow the adage "less is more." Except for its vine base, this wreath is made entirely of beech stems and leaves. Their grace and beauty alone suffice, requiring no further adornment. Begin by pressing a number of beech leaves between sheets of newspaper, but be sure to reserve some curled ones to use as accents. Moving around the wreath, glue beech twigs into the outer edge so that they radiate outward. Then cover the base with a layer of the flattened leaves. Using gaps between leaves to determine placement, glue a second set of twigs around the wreath. These should also radiate outward but face forward more than the first set. Using your eye as a guide, add smaller leaves and beechnuts until you have an arrangement that is just enough but not too much. ❧

Fresh from the Garden

However convincing the counterfeit, no matter how beautiful the dried flower, there is nothing to match the perfection of plants that are freshly cut. Fresh flowers, herbs, and foliage plants all wear a certain magic that is lost when they are dried, pressed, or otherwise preserved. Perhaps some of that magic derives from the fact that we know their glory is fleeting, and we enjoy them all the more because of their impermanence.

Imagine inviting your dinner guests to sample the centerpiece as one of the courses of their meal. This wreath is not only fresh, it is entirely edible (except for the base, of course). The herbs and flowers used here include parsley, oregano, thyme, fennel, dill, calendula, scented geranium, nasturtium, several mints, salad burnet, anise hyssop, rosemary, feverfew, chamomile, pineapple sage, kale, pansies, horehound, catnip, bay, sweet peas, and beet greens. To make your own, cut floral oasis to fit into a circular wire frame. After wetting the oasis thoroughly, insert the stems of your flowers and herbs directly into the base. The oasis will soak up the water and not leak a great deal, but you should protect your table with a piece of glass or plexiglass just to be safe. ∽

If you love fresh flowers and want a swag that will hold its beauty for more than a couple of days, choose this composition (opposite, top) with its small cluster of nerine lilies surrounded by a rosy halo of Peruvian lilies and radiating branches of lepto *(Leptospermum)*. All three flowers will dry beautifully in place. To make the base, start with a disassembled cinnamon broom that has been lightly sprayed with burgundy paint. Split the broom into two bunches, facing in opposite directions. Wire the bunches together in the center, and hot-glue a well-soaked bridal bouquet holder at the joint. With its handle removed, the bouquet holder makes a compact oasis to provide moisture to the fresh flowers. Insert a few sprigs of lepto to protect the bow from the moist oasis; then place a bow of pastel plaid ribbon in the center. Make a sharp, angular cut on each flower stem, and insert them directly into the bouquet holder. ∽

Winter's beauty and spring's promise are bound together in this lavish wreath (above). Curly mop-tops of bright red witch hazel are nestled into three varieties of cypress bush, together with some boxwood and hemlock. Nearby, fat rhododendron buds sit atop crimson stems of deep green leaves. Large, fluffy clumps of sedum anchor the arrangement, while branches of horsetail fly off in all directions around the edges. To construct this wreath, simply pick each of the plants into a small straw base. ∽

Fresh greenery is cool and refreshing any time of the year. In this asymmetrical arrangement (right), a thick arc of variegated pittosporum and berried eucalyptus is anchored at the bottom with a few galax leaves, and crowned at the top with a small fern. A second pittosporum, tendrils of ivy, and clusters of Spanish moss finish out the wreath. It is built upon a plastic-backed oasis base and requires only occasional misting to keep it fresh for days. Tiny bits of Spanish moss tucked between the plants hide the base from view. ∽

Artificials

Many an untrained eye has been fooled by realistic-looking faux materials. Some examples even have imperfections—brown edges on leaves, or pock marks on fruit—to make them appear all the more real. If you are devout in your commitment to natural materials, you had better turn the pages quickly. Otherwise, you may find yourself irresistibly tempted by these fascinating fakes.

A lush assortment of artificial fruit, flowers, and greenery makes a stunning wreath for display year-round or for special occasions. Because the materials are quite weather-worthy, this wreath is an ideal choice for an outside door or a garden gate if the ribbon can be protected from rain. It starts with an artificial laurel leaf garland attached to a wire wreath form, or you can purchase a wreath base made of artificial greenery. Make a bow of burgundy velvet ribbon, and glue it to the base. Using the bow as your starting point, position and hot-glue silk hydrangea blossoms and leaves, white-washed cones, artificial pomegranates, pears, plums, berry clusters, nuts, eucalyptus tips, and wild flowers to the base. It is easier to start with the larger items and fill in later with the smaller ones. Curl and loop an additional length of ribbon around the wreath, tucking it into and around the decorations. Hot-glue or wire the ribbon in place. ✿

Artificial flowers are the perfect solution when you need a garland that is colorful yet lightweight. A wide, wire-edged fabric ribbon, reinforced by the stems of the flowers, forms the base of the garland. Starting at one end, build your garland with a selection of fabric flowers that complement your furnishings. This one includes poppies, violets, roses, white heather, and pansies together with an upholstery-style floral design ribbon. Twist the stems together, and periodically wire the flowers to the ribbon. To make your garland complete, simply fluff the ribbon and adjust the positions of a few of the flowers. ∽

For a holiday wreath that will look handsome year after year despite being stored for several months in the closet, artificial greenery is ideal. A pine needle base, exposed on either side, adds a natural touch and coordinates well with the greens. Sprays of pine, variegated holly, and a cluster of berries are wired to the base at the top. These are followed by a few lengths of silk ivy picked and inserted around the edges. At the bottom, two clusters of red berries are wired to the base, with smaller stems of holly, pine, and ivy inserted around them. ✆

At a fraction of the cost of a long floral garland, you can create a dramatic visual effect on an open stairway by attaching a colorful swag to the newel post. Cut several pieces of twisted paper ribbon long enough to fit your newel post. This swag uses six pieces of pink ribbon and two of purple, but the numbers are not magical; use however many pieces necessary to create the thickness you like. Untwist the ribbon to open it fully. Next cut one length of paper lace ribbon and two of silk foliage. With all of the ribbons and greenery in hand, bind them together at the top and at the one-third and two-thirds points. Leave some slack in the paper between the binding points to create a look of fullness. After tying a bow of paper ribbon, make several loops of untwisted ribbon. Add a few to the bow, which is then attached to the top of the swag, and secure the others to the two lower points using chenille stems or twist ties. With the addition of a paper lace bow and some silk flowers and fruit at each point, this elegant swag is complete. ✍

Combining form and function, this wreath frames a small oval mirror that would be perfect in an entryway or master bedroom. These magnolia leaves will never curl and fade, nor will the plums shrivel to prunes; they, like the rest of the materials used here, are counterfeits. The base for this wreath is a purchased mirror framed in resilient foam, but you can substitute any mirror with a simple rounded frame. To disguise the construction and protect your wall, cover the back of the frame with fabric. Using a glue gun, attach the magnolia leaves to the frame, overlapping them slightly. Then glue six tips of artificial Canadian pine, two sprigs of bubble cedar, and a few stems of green berries in an arching spray formation at the bottom of the wreath. Loop a velvet ribbon into a bow, secure it with wire, and glue it in place on the spray. Two artificial plums and a pomegranate add the finishing touch. ⌒

Mix 'n' Match

*Purism may work for some, but there is no rule that says
naturals can't be combined with fakes. Sometimes it's a matter
of convenience or availability; other times, you may not want
to sacrifice permanence for a purely natural appearance.
Whatever the reason, if you're after a certain effect or
composition that just happens to include some of everything,
don't look back over your shoulder. Press on ahead, and
remember, if such rules do exist, they're made to be broken!*

Birch branches create an airy base for this simple yet sophisticated swag. The branches are layered with stems of ti tree, then wired together in the middle. After a full, casual bow made of raffia is tied into the center, individual stems of silk flowers are inserted on either side. These can be secured with hot glue if necessary. A large sponge mushroom and a cluster of pods are hot-glued beneath the bow, and a pair of silk blossoms with their foliage is attached in the center. ↷

Although most wreaths are circular, a spectacular effect can be achieved with something altogether different. Here a filigree of bent twigs forms a square base for an off-center spray of fernlike foliage and artificial fruit. Such bases can be purchased or constructed from supple young whips of grapevine, willow, or other flexible wood. On the lower right corner, hot-glue a few tips of preserved plumosa, followed by a stem or two of artificial bean pods with foliage. Add a cluster of artificial pomegranates and a loose raffia bow. At the top, wind a long stem of bean pods and foliage through the lacy frame, and hot-glue it in place. Add one last stem of plumosa and a feathered bird to complete the arrangement. ∞

Artificial fruit can be equal in drama to flowers. These ripe pomegranates, bursting forth with seeds, are the center of attention in this woodland swag. The base is a frame of grapevines, cut and curved into interlocking arches. To secure the stems of artificial pomegranates and silk artichokes, twist them into the vine and glue them in place. Add stems of canella berries and dried sarracenia, some additional artificial foliage, and a tree fungus on top and bottom. Glue on bits of lichen to fill any gaps. One included here has a dried mushroom attached. ∽

Thanks to artificials, even those living in northern climates can experience the exuberance of magnolia blossoms. Here they are paired with several sprays of fresh pussy willow and a stem of artificial crab apples. The stems are all inserted into a square of foam that has been well covered with Spanish moss. As a finishing touch, a piece of tree fungus, hot-glued to a pick, is inserted on one side of the flowers. ∽

Living Wreaths & Swags

Most compositions, by their nature, are static in appearance. Only a living swag or wreath can offer a new scene from day to day. With a little forethought, you can create pockets large enough in your base to accommodate enough potting soil to support a variety of foliage and blossoming plants. A word of caution: when you water your plants, remove the swag or wreath from the wall, or you will soon have a nice puddle on the floor below.

Branches of contorted fig form an artistic trellis for the outstretching tendrils of ivy. To make a similar arrangement, take several curly branches of fig or willow, and wire them together.

You may need to attach a block of foam to give the assembly stability and a flat surface to rest against a wall. Next, wire and glue a small basket to the lower center of the branches. Add some pot-

ting soil, and plant several ivy cuttings and an African violet in the basket. If you included a block of foam on your base, be sure to cover it with sheet moss so that it doesn't show. ☜

60

The heralds of spring, flowering bulbs are sure to lift any spirits sagging from a case of the winter blahs. And they are ideal for making a living wreath. Because bulbs have their own self-contained source of nourishment, they need little or no soil and only a regular misting to keep the flowers fresh. This springtime symphony begins with a large vine base whose sizable interior spaces are filled with Spanish moss. The three hyacinths are placed first, followed by the tulips. Each bulb is carefully wrapped with moss to protect its roots while the plant is positioned into the wreath. Similarly, individual ivy plants are removed from their small pots, their soil wrapped in moss, and inserted all around the wreath. A large, complementary bow adds a cheerful touch at the bottom. ‰

Six weeks after planting.

Immediately after planting.

Houseleeks, more affectionately known as "hens and chicks," are one of the most satisfying plants you can use for a living wreath. These members of the sedum family grow almost before your eyes, and each "hen" produces so many "chicks" that you may be tempted to make several wreaths to hold them all! Build your base from chicken wire, shaping it into a circle, square, heart, or whatever shape you desire. After lining it with sphagnum moss, fill the form with potting soil. Plant the sedums well apart to give them room to grow and multiply. Press each plant firmly into the soil, and cover the soil with pieces of sheet moss. Finally, spiral a fine-gauge wire all around the wreath to hold everything in place, making sure not to wire across the plants. ∽

For the look of a miniature garden, combine a half-dozen of your favorite plants into a single swag. This one includes several pansies, New Guinea impatiens, wandering Jew, firecracker plant, sedum, and lantana. To make a sturdy base, cut a piece of thick plywood the size and shape you want. Then cut a piece of chicken wire in the same general shape, but significantly larger than your base. You want to make a pocket for your plants and will need enough extra chicken wire to fold back over their roots. Wrap each plant's roots and soil in sheet moss, and secure the bundle with a floral pin or twist tie. After stapling the chicken wire onto the plywood, place your plants on the base. Fold the chicken wire back over the plants, securing it with a few staples if necessary. A few clumps of Spanish moss hide the chicken wire from view. ∽

Fall Harvest

*A brisk nip in the air and the crunch of fallen leaves
underfoot help to quicken the step, reminding us
that the days are shortening and there is much to be done
before the onset of winter. No matter that more of us now
work with computers than with threshers and balers;
our agrarian roots have instilled a seasonal clock
deep within our psyche. Autumn is the time for
finishing up those projects begun during
the endless days of summer, taking stock for
the upcoming winter, and giving thanks
for the bounty of the season's harvest.*

What more genuine a welcome can you offer arriving guests than the sight of a harvest wreath hanging by the door? This one utilizes a purchased base made from a tropical vine, but you can build a similar base from thick, heavy grapevines. To decorate it, make bundles of broomcorn, winter rye, and sorghum, wrapping each with floral tape. Insert these into the vines across the top half of the wreath, and secure them in place with hot glue. Then add a trio of strawberry corn on each side and a cluster of dried pomegranates at the bottom center. To fill in the spaces between, tuck moistened corn shucks, stems of rose hips, preserved oak leaves, and okra pods into the vines. Small pine cones glued here and there make the finishing touch. ∽

64

Warm, rich tones of brown mark this autumnal wreath. Glycerine-preserved leaves are pinned and glued to the straw base to make a full, textured ground for the contrasting nuts, seeds, and flowers. To create its full appearance, bundles of leaves still on their original stems, are packed tightly onto the wreath. Intermittently around the wreath, walnuts, sprays of artificial acorns, and snippets of baby's breath are glued in place. ∞

Throughout history, wheat has symbolized the abundance of harvest time. In addition to providing the basis for much of our food, wheat is a handsome material for decorating the home. This swag, made of wheat and phalaris (a grass), is perfect for a front door, and it is resilient enough to be used year after year. After dividing the wheat and grass into three bundles of each, cluster the grass so that its tops extend just beyond the wheat heads. You now have three combined bundles. Without cutting the stems, attach the three bunches to one another with floral-taped wire. Leave enough of the stems exposed between the bunches to allow for the bows. Make three bows, each with long streamers, and run the streamers from the top bow down to the second, and from the second to the third. After everything is secured, trim the stems and ribbon streamers at the bottom. ∞

The strong diagonal sweep formed by a sheaf of wheat is emphasized by the gentle curve of a long oval vine base. With its convoluted twists and turns and shaggy bark, the vine itself becomes an important element in the design. Grounding the wheat to the base of the wreath is a piece of tree fungus, clumps of moss, and a few of the season's last roses. All are glued in place, as are the clusters of pepperberries arrayed about the wreath. A raffia bow glued to the top adds a casual finishing touch. ✎

Flowers and berries in vivid reds, punctuated by blossoms of brassy gold, are interwoven with the muted grays and browns of dried flowers, mosses, fruits, and pods in a tapestry of fall color. To make this wreath, assemble dried pomegranates, poppy seed heads, dried marigold, sarracenia, globe amaranth, nandina berries, rose hips, and a variety of tree fungi and mosses. Then, using hot glue, attach them onto an unruly, somewhat oval base of honeysuckle vines and pine twigs. The arrangement should be casual, with more or less of the bright fall colors, however the eye dictates. ☙

Holiday Celebrations

Every family has its own holiday traditions. For some, Christmas truly arrives only when the tree ornaments are first unpacked. Others could not imagine an Easter without mixing dyes and making decorated eggs. And everyone knows the joy of receiving a valentine from someone special. We can channel our creative urges to recreate familiar images from our childhood or to build new visions of important traditions.

Nothing evokes the warm feelings of Christmas quite so effectively as a traditional evergreen wreath with its broad red ribbon. Depending on your preferences, you can construct this wreath with natural or artificial greenery. To build a quick evergreen base, wind a garland of fir or spruce around a wire wreath form, securing it periodically with wire. Flatten a spot on the greens, and wire a small, square piece of foam onto the base. You can disguise the foam by gluing sheet moss over it. Using about four yards (3.5 m) of velvet ribbon, tie a bow and pick it into the foam. Then pick four natural mahogany pods and approximately two feet (61 cm) of silk grape-leaf ivy into the foam. To add color and texture, wind a few red berry tips onto the ends of the silk ivy, and attach pine cone rosettes in a few locations around the wreath. For a whimsical touch, glue or wire a red-feathered bird onto one of the branches. ❧

This cheerful holiday swag is a perfect project for those left-over boughs of evergreen that are too numerous to throw away but not sufficient for making an entire wreath. Start with a handful of grapevines twisted together and curved into a gentle arch. Then insert stems of your greenery into the nooks and crannies of the grapevine. With fresh materials, there is no need to glue or wire the stems in place. They should wedge in tightly enough to hold through the holiday season, and you can remove them afterward to re-use the arch base later. If you use artificial greens, as shown here, you may want to add a bit of hot glue for reinforcement and permanence. Tie each pine cone onto a dainty ivory ribbon by sliding the ribbon underneath the bottom few petals of the cone, making a knot, and covering the knot with a few snippets of greenery. After arranging the ribbons so that the cones hang at varying levels, wire them onto the center of the swag, together with a few lengths cut from a gold snowflake garland. Tie a bow with wire-edged grosgrain ribbon, using a contrasting ribbon to make streamers, and wire it in place. As a final touch, insert a cluster of berries on either side of the bow. ✑

A silvery halo of Spanish moss offers a pleasing contrast to a festive mix of crab apples, also known as "love apples," and galax leaf clusters. The wreath is made by pinning moss over the entire surface of a plastic-covered straw base. Taking three galax leaves at a time, pick the clusters in place at several locations around the wreath. To attach the apples, poke a wire through the lower side of each apple near the blossom end, and wrap the wire around a pick. Pick in small clusters of dyed baby's breath (available at craft stores), and attach a burgundy velvet bow for drama. For a bit of gloss, rub a little vegetable oil onto the leaves and apples. ❧

73

For a less conventional approach, the beauty of the grapevine base can become an important element in your composition. Here, a generous mass of blue cedar, white pine, and fir is wired to the base, followed by a decorative bow of metallic and satin sheen ribbon. Finally, two stems of artificial berries—one sprayed silver—are tucked in alongside the bow. ☙

A heart within a circle—everlasting love in any language—is a perfect keepsake for your favorite Valentine. The heart is made from a few twists of gilded vine, bent around into an easy heart, with the joint covered by a delicate ribbon bow, a spray of hydrangea, and a single dried rose. Two tiny bouquets of hydrangea, a stem of pepperberries, and a casual twist of ribbon provide an asymmetrical accent. The circular foam base is wrapped in a sumptuous floral ribbon and embellished with a three-loop bow of the same ribbon, three rose buds, and a small clutch of hydrangea. The ends of the ribbon are left long to be knotted, twisted, and draped along the sides of the wreath. ❧

75

What a hearty welcome for your neighborhood trick-or-treaters! This jolly pumpkin man was purchased, but you could make your own papier-mâché figure to greet your Halloween guests. Glue and wire him into a large straw wreath, using a noose of fine wire to secure him at the top. (You can cover the wire around his neck with a piece of raffia tied into a bow.) Using a glue gun, attach a mini-bale of hay and a tiny pumpkin near his feet, filling in with preserved oak leaves. Assemble two sprays of wheat, cattails, and okra pod stems, and wire them—one facing up and the other down—alongside one edge of the wreath. Hide the wire with a purple paper ribbon bow. Glue a miniature clay pot under the arm of the pumpkin man, add some raffia for hands, and hot-glue a few leaves spilling out of the clay pot. ∞

Brightly colored Easter eggs wait to be discovered as they rest among a bed of amaranths, roses, and marigolds. Begin with an oval base of grapevines, and glue half a dozen small pads of sheet moss and Spanish moss randomly around the base. Concentrating the deco-ration in the lower right quadrant, glue on several small bunches of spike ama-ranth and marigolds and a few perfect roses. Work in bits of ambrosia and more spike amaranth and marigolds, diminishing the concentra-tion as you move outward from the lower right. Fill in any bare spots with statice and globe amaranth, sprin-kling small bits of both across the top of the wreath. Position and glue the eggs in place, and give them a more settled appearance by adding a few more flowers nearby. ∽

Heavenly Scents

Most swags, garlands, and wreaths are designed to please the eye, but why stop there? More than any other, our sense of smell has the ability to evoke our deepest emotions. A whiff of fragrance that reminds us of a special occasion can return us instantly to that moment. When determining your composition, use scent as you would any other design element: as a subtle accent or a major focus.

With its heady aroma, a wreath of preserved eucalyptus will not go unnoticed in any room. The fragrance subsides over time, but never altogether disappears. To make a wreath that is as handsome in appearance as it is in scent, combine the deep blue-green foliage with bright white sand dollars and smooth, gothic-looking miter shells. Prepare bunches of eucalyptus, three stems to a bunch, that are four or five inches (10-13 cm) long. To make picking them easier, remove the bottom two leaves from each stem. Insert the eucalyptus in a spiral around the inside of a straw wreath base and in a double spiral around the outside. To attach the sand dollars, cut four chenille stems in half, insert one half into the inside slit of each sand dollar, and gently twist the stem together below the shell. Wire the stems to picks, and place the shells evenly around the wreath. After removing the wires from eight picks, hot-glue one pick into the base opening of each miter shell. While the glue is setting, fill in between sand dollars with more bunches of eucalyptus so that the shells cannot rub against one another. Insert the miter shells between the sand dollars to create an alternating pattern.

Flowers Noted for Their Fragrance

Depending on which species they belong to, flowers can vary considerably in their levels of fragrance. Some also have a wide range of scents. Determining what they smell like, or if their perfume is desirable, is strictly a matter of individual taste. No two noses will ever gain exactly the same impression. These are some flowers with a noticeable scent; it's up to you to decide which you most enjoy.

Bee balm	*Mock orange*
Candytuft	*Nasturtium*
Clematis	*Peony*
Daffodil	*Pinks*
Freesia	*Rose*
Grape hyacinth	*Scented geranium*
Honeysuckle	*Stock*
Hyacinth	*Sweet Annie*
Jasmine	*Sweet pea*
Lavender	*Tansy*
Lilac	*Tulip*
Lily	*Viburnum*
Lily of the valley	*Violet*
Marigold	*Wisteria*

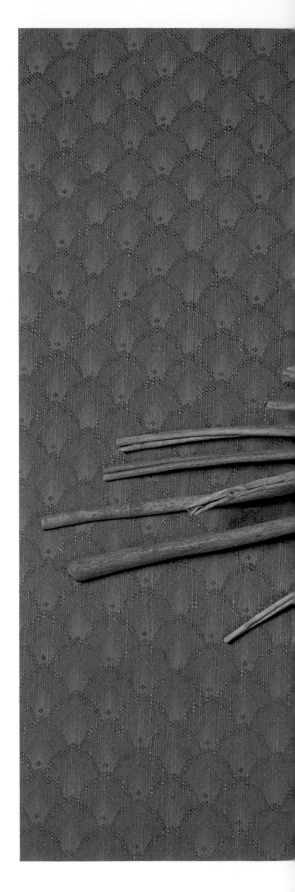

For a spicy scent that brings back warm memories of grandmother's homemade apple pie fresh out of the oven, create a swag that includes a liberal number of giant cinnamon sticks and dried apple slices. Start with a block of moss-covered foam, and insert the cinnamon sticks so they radiate out from the center. Arrange the cinnamon in three layers from back to front to give the swag fullness. Then hot-glue dried apple slices on top and between the layers of cinnamon sticks. As a colorful garnish, glue a bunch of artificial cranberries in the center. On the back of the swag, glue palm leaves trimmed into a neat wedge shape. (*Hint:* Cinnamon sticks vary greatly in their level of fragrance; if yours are lacking, wipe on a few drops of cinnamon oil to give them a boost.) ∽

To make a festive table wreath that is not only beautiful to look at but has a heavenly fragrance, gather a selection of scented geraniums: peppermint, staghorn oak, and rose. Push the leaf stems into a moistened oasis ring that has been wired to maintain its shape. To create a lush, verdant setting, add trailing rosemary and lemon verbena. The vivid red accents consist of pineapple sage (the tubular blossoms), red celosia, and a few fresh strawflowers. The deep lavender blooms are Mexican bush sage. With a trio of red candles, this wreath makes a stunning centerpiece, and if kept cool when not being used, it will still look fresh more than a week later. ✄

It's easy to drift into dreamland when you are lulled by the soft floral scent of sweet Annie, lavender, and roses. These fragrant blooms decorate a wreath that is built upon a base of flared birch branches. Such bases are available in craft shops, but you can easily make your own if you have a birch tree available. Begin decorating the base by hot-gluing six-inch(15 cm) tips of sweet Annie around the wreath, placing the base of the stems about an inch (2.5 cm) apart, and flaring the tips outward on an angle. After misting them with water, hot-glue stems of baby's breath around the center of the wreath. Follow this with about a dozen bunches of lavender and ten dried red roses evenly spaced all around. Finally, cut and pick eight short strands of simulated pearls into the wreath, forming generous, diagonal loops. ❧

Wedding Presents

*When the bride is a good friend and/or a member of the family,
a wedding wreath makes a lasting memento of that glorious
occasion. For those fortunate enough to host a wedding,
it is easier than you think to construct a magnificent
garland to provide a triumphant entrance for the bride.
If you lack the appropriate stairway, simply
adjust the length and quantity of materials
to make an equally attractive arch
to position over a doorway.*

Flowers have long been given meanings apart from their loveliness, and no culture has ever used that hidden language more effectively and eloquently than the Victorians. A heart-shaped wreath graced with appropriate herbs and flowers speaks of love in its beauty and its meaning.

For this wreath, begin with a heart-shaped wire frame. Wrap the frame with scraps of artemisia stems to give it bulk, and secure them in place with monofilament spiralled around several times. Again using monofilament, attach four-inch (10 cm) pieces of artemisia blossoms around the base. Finally, hot-glue the decorative flowers onto the artemisia, starting at the top and ending at the base, matching the flowers on either side. This wreath includes blue salvia (I think of you), carnations (bonds of affection), celosia (affection), globe amaranth (immortality), lavender (devotion), marjoram (joy and happiness), nigella (love-in-a-mist), roses (love), rosemary (remembrance), and thyme (courage). ∽

To make this wreath, use a 13-inch (33 cm) heart-shaped straw base. Cut 25 pieces of white paper ribbon, each eight inches (20 cm) long. After spreading them open, pinch them in the center, wire them to picks, and attach them around the outer edge of the base to form a continuous ruffle. Make small bouquets of artemisia, and attach them around the inside of the heart with floral pins. Work in one direction, placing each bunch so that it covers the pin for the previous bouquet. Repeat this process along the outside rim of the wreath base—above the paper ribbon ruffle—to establish a visual frame for the herbs and flowers. (*Hint*: To make it easier to insert the final bunch under the first, tape the ends of the artemisia to the pick.) Misting the herbs with water makes them more flexible. Moving around the wreath, attach small bouquets of eac flower, balancing the colors and textures.

The flowers and herbs included here are: amaranth (immortality), bay (glory), baby's breath (gaiety), chamomile (patience), celosia (affection), everlastings (never ceasing remembrance), hyssop (loving sacrifice), lavender (devotion), oregano (substance), rosemary (your presence revives me), rose (love), spearmint (warm feelings), savory (interest), thyme (courage), and yarrow (dreams of a loved one). ∽

Any bride would be thrilled to make her entrance down a stairway that is graced by a garland of wild roses in pink and white. The flowers look as if they were freshly picked for the occasion, but are in fact artificial. To make a total length of 12 feet (3.5 m), four shorter garlands of the pink roses and three of the white are intertwined with silk ivy. Just wind the stems together, twisting them several times to make a spine that won't fall apart as you maneuver it. When the flowers and foliage are arranged to your liking, thread a wired ribbon lazily through the garland. Pinch the ribbon here and there, securing it onto the foliage. ∽

Table-Toppers

Sitting atop a table rather than hugging a wall, a wreath or swag offers a whole new viewing perspective. The fact that it will be seen from many different angles poses new opportunities and challenges. You no longer need to worry about gravity pulling your design out of shape, and you can use strong vertical elements to create a dynamic composition. At the same time, you must remember to devote equal attention all around; only the bottom will be hidden from view.

An abundance of color marks this tabletop garden. It is built on a straw base that has been pulled into an oval shape. (To protect a fine wood table, it is wise to retain the green plastic covering on the base.) Create your own garden scene by starting with the main vertical components: silk tulips and dried fern on one side, and dried marigolds and eucalyptus on the other. Moving from the edges toward the center, pick in the silk violets and pansies, and hot-glue several mushrooms and pieces of tree fungus onto the base. Glue on an assortment of mahogany pods, and fill in any gaps with yellow strawflowers, globe amaranth, and German statice. Around the bottom edges of the base, attach silk hydrangea leaves. To mimic nature's touch, glue on a lichen-covered twig as if it has fallen amidst the flowers. ✑

Luscious fruit mingled with fresh flowers make a wreath guaranteed to knock the socks off your dinner guests. To create one of your own, start with the vibrant colors: a pair of fiery red roses, a deep purple iris, and magenta carnations. Cut the stems very short and insert them into a well-soaked oasis ring. (If you use the type that has a plastic backing, your table will be protected from dampness.) Fill in the sides with clusters of red grapes, some berried eucalyptus, and a few branches of variegated pittosporum. For the heavier clusters of grapes, use floral pins to anchor them. Thread a glitzy ribbon around the wreath by wiring it at various locations to picks and inserting the picks into the oasis. Now add the softer colors: violet statice, and rosy pink nerine lilies and spring asters. For a whimsical touch, slice a lime in half, jab the halves onto picks, and add them to your composition. ∽

All of the peace and serenity of an afternoon's walk in the woods are captured in this woodland swag. It is tailored to fit a long, narrow sofa table, but you can alter the size and shape to fit your desired location. Start with a very heavy piece of wire bent to the shape you want. (The wire should be about three times the thickness of a coat hanger, or you can use plywood cut to shape instead.) Build up the form with straw, wrapping it with wire or monofilament to hold the straw in place. Be sure to keep one side flat so that it will sit firmly on your table. Attach the larger clumps of moss with floral pins, and hot-glue the other materials. Use pieces of tree fungus, lichen-covered stones and twigs, and dried mushrooms to create micro-environments within your composition. For accents, include dried celosia in muted tones of gold and terra-cotta and a couple of dried sarracenia blooms. ❧

Bed & Bath

Wreaths and swags have come a long way since they were confined to the front door to mark the holiday season. Now you can find beautiful examples gracing every room of the house, including the master bedroom and bath. In the bedroom, the choice of materials is infinite; select whatever colors and textures best enhance your decor. For a bathroom, color is a strong consideration, but durability is equally important if the room is regularly subjected to high levels of moisture from bathing.

For a truly elegant look in a refined boudoir setting, choose a selection of dried flowers and herbs coupled with a lush velvet ribbon. This gentle arch begins with three-foot (91 cm) sections of grapevine wired together to make the desired thickness. Bunches of silvery gray artemisia form the background for accents of anise hyssop and Russian sage. The ribbon is added next, and the open loops are formed by gathering the ribbon onto picks at six locations along its length.

A dab of hot glue on each pick helps secure the ribbon onto the vine base. Broad, mustard-yellow heads of yarrow are glued and picked at each point where the ribbon is gathered. Additional color is provided by clusters of salvia victoria, two shades of pink globe amaranth, feverfew, crested celosia, and strawflowers. The arch can be sprayed with a sealer to preserve it, and it can be periodically misted with water to help keep it from shedding. ∞

It's easy to choose not only colors that harmonize with your decorating scheme, but materials as well. Here, the whitewashed vine base neatly complements the turned open-work on the bed frame. To make a striking composition, all that needs to be added are a handful of roses, a bouquet of larkspur, and a simple bow. Wire or glue the flowers in place, and glue the bow on top. Be sure not to cut the stems if you want to keep the dramatic diagonal line. ∽

Reflecting the casual mood of the room, a braided swag over the vanity mirror adds just the right touch. To make your own, measure three pieces of natural colored paper ribbon the length you want for the total swag, adding a bit extra to accommodate bows and braiding. Cut four equal lengths of 18-gauge wire to include in the braid as reinforcement. Begin braiding about eight inches (20 cm) from the top, and stop the same distance short from the end. At the center and at each end, attach bows made of paper ribbon and raffia. In the middle of each bow, glue dried apple slices, tiny pine cones, statice, and cinnamon sticks. ∞

Sapphire blue highlights amidst a myriad of rose pinks add drama to a quiet corner of the bedroom. Mounted on a single wire ring, silver king artemisia forms the base for an opulent floral wreath.

Use scraps of artemisia stems, and wrap them onto a wire ring. Finish the base with finer tips of artemisia and dried grasses, facing them outward from the center. In a single spiral around the top surface, glue roses, carnations, blue thistle, caspia, pepperberries, and blue salvia. Also include mini-bouquets of larkspur, celosia, globe amaranth, nigella, hydrangea, strawflowers, and zinnias. ∽

Dried herbs are an excellent choice for the bathroom because the moisture will release their fragrance and help prevent shedding. To make a curved arch, cut a large straw wreath base in half, and bind off the loose ends. Beginning at the ends and working toward the center, use fern pins to apply bunches of silver king artemisia to the form. Finish the outer rims first; then fill in the center. Cut a three-foot (91 cm) length of wired ribbon, and pin it to the center of the arch so that approximately the same amount of ribbon dangles loosely on either side. Form a large bow, secure it with wire, and attach it over the pinned center of the streamers. Before securing the streamers, create your color overlay by applying clusters of anise hyssop and flower heads of crested celosia, strawflowers, and yarrow. Now lift the ribbon streamers to form curves that extend gracefully above and below the center line of the flower overlay. Pin the ribbon in place, and fill in any spaces with additional strawflowers. A fixative spray will help keep your creation looking beautiful. ∽

For a crisp designer look, place this simple swag (below) over a towel rack or medicine cabinet. It is made with curly ting-ting, caspia, and bell cup pods, all purchased in a color to match linens or other bath accessories. Divide a bunch of curly ting-ting in half, arrange the curly ends opposite each other, and bind the swag together with floral-taped wire. (The tape helps hold the wire in place.) After making a bow of stiff lace ribbon, attach it and the bell cup pods into the center. Lastly, glue some pieces of caspia into the bow and on either side. ∽

Colorful wallpaper in the guest lavatory calls for something strong and solid that can hold its own (opposite). The braided wheat, raffia, and artificial grapes are good choices to withstand moisture, but if the room is often used for bathing, the paper ribbon bow may eventually discolor. Braided wheat purchased at a craft shop (or constructed if you are nimble of finger) can be easily wound onto a single wire ring. Using a long needle and strong upholstery or buttonhole thread, sew the braid onto the ring. Make a simple country bow from creamy white paper ribbon, glue on a few peach raffia streamers, and wire it through the wheat onto the base ring. After positioning the grape stems, wire them in place. ∽

98

Miniatures

When you're finished with your major projects, never throw away your extra bits and pieces; they're perfect for making pint-sized wreaths for gifts or for yourself. You'll be amazed at how versatile they are. Pretty soon you'll be using them for everything from personal adornment to tacking up notices on the family refrigerator. And they're very quick to make. In under an hour you can easily construct a tiny magnet wreath or napkin ring. These are but a few examples of where wreath miniatures can shine; let your imagination be your guide.

With only a modicum of effort and materials, you can make a matching set of napkin rings and candle holders that will impress even the most discriminating guest. For the nap-kin rings, make four—or six, or eight—vine bases about three inches (8 cm) in diameter. Decorate each a little differently, using a glue gun to attach silk flowers, miniature greenery, and dried grasses. Don't go overboard with your decorations; it's much easier to insert the napkins into the rings if you leave much of the vine base exposed. ☙

For the matching candle rings, build two vine bases that are both about six inches (15 cm) in outside diameter. Then, with your glue gun, add the same or similar flowers that you used for the napkin rings. This pair includes some German statice and a few bay leaves in addition to the silk flowers, greenery, and dried grasses. When decorating your candle rings, keep in mind that these wreaths will be displayed horizontally. Arrange your flowers and greens at varying levels to result in greater depth and visual interest. ∞

This collection of wreath magnets certainly adds class to the family 'fridge. Each starts with a five-inch (13 cm) artificial evergreen base (available in craft shops) that is flattened and trimmed. The top wreath is first covered with preserved cedar; then small branches of plumed and crested celosia, pearly everlasting, and baby's breath are arranged in concentric circles and glued in place. To make the middle magnet, hot-glue bay leaves onto the base, followed by an arrangement of dried pansies, santolina blossoms, and sprigs of caspia. For the wreath on the bottom, cut short tips of artemisia about 1-1/2 to two inches (4–5 cm) long, and glue them around the outside. Follow this with a thick ring of strawflower clusters. On the inside of the circle, glue nine miniature rosebuds all around, making sure that each stem is covered by the following bud. Finish each wreath by hot-gluing three small circular magnets equally spaced onto the back of the evergreen base. ❧

While the ancients often wore wreaths on their heads as symbols of honor and achievement, you can wear yours on your heart purely as decoration. A honeysuckle wreath made into a pin is a natural accompaniment to a cotton sweater. With glue gun in hand, simply attach several blossoms around the lower two-thirds of the circle. Those used here include various everlastings, statice, tansy, and strawflowers, but any assortment will look pretty. Finish by gluing on a bow made of narrow satin ribbon, embellished with a couple of flower tops. ∽

103

With Birds in Mind

According to current statistics, bird watching and feeding are second in popularity only to gardening as a pastime. Feeding time antics are more entertaining than local television, and nothing is more thrilling than a close encounter with a large bird on the wing. Wreath makers, too, have found many ways to express their admiration of these feathered creatures. Here are but a few examples.

Birds and their homes provide the major focal point for this three-ringed swag (or triple wreath, if you prefer). Make three vine circles of equal size, wire them together at their edges, and spray them with a light coat of varnish to impart a moderate sheen. Collect a few pieces of bark from a fallen limb (not from a live tree!) to use as platforms for the birds and small houses. Wedge the ends of the bark pieces into the vines, and attach them with plenty of hot glue at the desired locations. Glue the houses and the birds onto the bark, followed by pieces of ming fern arranged to look like small pine trees. Finally, attach some silk roses and bits of lichen. ✂

If you are fortunate enough to come upon an abandoned bird's nest, it makes a distinctive focal point for a wreath. This nest-within-a-nest is so enticing it has already attracted a colorful pair. To make the basket-shaped base, start with two grapevine circles, one six inches (15 cm) and the other nine inches (23 cm) in diameter. Cut five twigs, each about four inches (10 cm) long, to use as spokes to join the two circles. Then, using just enough hot glue on the spokes to hold the circles together, weave in additional grapevine to make the sides. Turn the basket on its side, and wire your treasured find into a comfortable spot. Make a corona of horehound stems, glue your birds in place, and add final touches of purple statice and everlasting blossoms. ∽

In addition to their forsaken nests, woodland birds leave behind many remnants of their lives among the tall trees. This "witches' broom" of twiggy hawthorne, moss, pressed leaves, tree fungi, a wasp's nest, and assorted nuts, pods, and cones makes an ideal setting for a tiny wren's skull nestled at the top. The wreath base is made of grapevine, and the materials are all hot-glued in place. A few trial runs to establish the composition, especially for the more significant items, may be needed before gluing. To dry your own beech and ginkgo leaves (the golden, fan-shaped ones), place them between sheets of newspaper. If you include an abandoned wasp or bee's nest, be sure to bake it in the oven for several minutes to avoid any unwanted confrontations. ✑

Clusters of small bird nests (purchased at a craft store) add a special touch to this magnificent wreath. It starts with a straw wreath base covered with moss that you can collect from the forest floor or purchase in sheets from a floral supplier. Alder twigs, complete with their seed pods, radiate from the outer edge of the covered base. Small branches and individual leaves from a magnolia tree, galax leaves, and Virginia pine cones are picked into strategic locations. To finish out the natural look, crab apples and Seckel pears are wired in place. ∞

For an interactive experience, build a wreath that the birds can enjoy too. Hanging from a limb, it offers the best of all possible worlds: a place to perch and eat at the same time! The wreath is actually a spiral, a continuous circle that never closes. It is made from wire-reinforced grapevine and covered with ropes of millet. Short strands of raffia hold the millet on the wreath. Suspended by wire wrapped with brown floral tape, a peanut butter and birdseed bell hangs in the middle. (You can find millet ropes at pet shops, and molded birdseed bells at local grocery stores.) To add a bit of decoration—and another treat for the birds—a small sheaf of wheat is attached at the top, and a few dried flowers are tucked into points along the spiral. ∽

Children's Corner

Garlands, wreaths, and swags are no longer the exclusive province of adults. Infants and children of all ages will delight in room decorations that incorporate favored themes or toys. In one combined motion, you can tidy up the toy box and construct a piece with plenty of child appeal. Alternatively, a collection of small toys and other goodies made into a wreath or garland is a novel gift.

A wreath of infant bottles, toys, and a pair of lacy dress-up shoes makes a perfect gift for the new mother. She can disengage the contents for the baby's immediate enjoyment or use it as a decoration to dress up the nursery. To make the wreath, start with a foam ring wrapped with wide satin ribbon. Using a narrow pastel ribbon, tie a bow onto the ring holding a set of baby rattles, and another around the necks of two colorful infant bottles. Then secure each with floral pins to either side of the base. Insert the broad end of a pick into the bottom of a rubber duck, and anchor the duck to the wreath with a little hot glue. With a piece of white satin ribbon secured at the top, dangle a pair of shoes in the center. Finish by gluing additional ribbons and bows along the sides and at the top. ∽

Rocking baby to sleep is all part of the fun when the cradle is decked with a garland complete with a teddy bear and his friends. Colorful, interlocking chewing rings appear to connect the toys. In fact, they are attached to a thin vine arch for stability, and allowed to dangle free at one end. The vines are twined together, bound at each end, and painted with a light spray of nontoxic white paint. A twist of wire connects the bear at one end of the arch and the duck at the other. In the center, a soft frog rattle is attached at a jaunty angle. Tricolored bows made of narrow satin ribbon are worn by all. ∽

Here a jolly duo of hand puppets joins forces with a stuffed bull whose shifty eyes and rakish grin are sure to bring a smile to all. This wreath is also accommodating to youthful demands; the puppets are mounted on coat hangers and can be removed for "one last show," then replaced when their performance is complete. It starts with a flat-sided foam base wrapped with satin ribbon. To mount the puppets, cut and twist the coat hangers so that their curved tops hold the puppet heads erect. Floral wire secures a colorful bow and holds the bull in check. ❧

In this cheery scene, miniature dolls and bunny rabbits dance merrily around in a circle, joined by other childhood delights. These can all be purchased at craft shops, then decorated using paint pens or small brushes. The wreath base is a simple 16-inch (41 cm) "donut" sewn from pink, blue, and yellow plaid fabric, and filled with polyester fiber. Small "bows" are actually butterfly shapes cut from the same fabric. They are tacked to the base with a few stitches; then each is decorated with a colorful pin head glued in the middle. (Don't be tempted to use real pins; they can be dangerous in the hands of small children.) A wide ribbon cut and hemmed makes a large bow at the bottom. ✑

If discarded toys are too shabby to use as decorative elements in your composition, don't despair. A hand-crafted, country-style bear is a ready substitute with equal charm. Once the bear is settled into the center of a lightly white-washed vine wreath, all you need to add is a few sprays of German statice, clusters of pepperberries, and a fabric ribbon bow to harmonize with your decor. Use a glue gun to secure the bear and his embellishments. ∽

Culinary Delights

For as long as humans have cultivated the soil to produce fruits and vegetables, staples such as garlic and onions have been strung together for storage and to hang within reach of the cook-stove. Somewhere along the line, someone discovered that this custom was not only practical, but beautiful. Today, foodstuffs make some of the most attractive—and mouth-watering—decorative elements you can use for your compositions.

A bountiful fruit wreath enlivens your entry or front door, and cool weather will keep it fresh for weeks. It does make a heavy display, though, and requires a stiff wire hanger and a solid nail. The first step is to fasten the pineapple in the center of a straw wreath that has been covered with clusters of boxwood. Using a piece of 1/8- to 1/4-inch (3–6 mm) diameter bamboo that is long enough to reach across the lower quarter of the wreath, drive the stake through the sides of the pineapple near its bottom. Hide the ends of the bamboo by pushing them into the wreath form, and secure them in place with wire. Then make a wire noose around the leafy crown of the pineapple, and lash the loose end of the wire around the top of the wreath. To fill in the sides, select an assortment of fresh fruit, nuts, and berries. Heavier fruits such as apples can be fastened in place by pushing two wires at right angles through the bottom sides of each fruit. To attach nuts, drill a small hole in one end using a 1/16-inch (1.5 mm) bit, add a drop of hot glue, and insert a wire. Cranberry clusters are created by wiring individual cranberries and wrapping the wires onto a pick. ✑

Short culinary swags are a delightful addition to your kitchen, and they cost very little to make. If you spray them with a fixative (sealer), they should keep their color and shape for months.

This one displays dried key lime and clove pomanders, whole bay leaves, cinnamon sticks, and dried apple and orange slices mounted on a braid of lemongrass. To make the braid, gather 20-inch-long (51 cm) strands of lemongrass into three bunches each about the size of your thumb. Wire them together about three inches (8 cm) from the top, and form a hanging loop. Braid the lemongrass, wiring it at the bottom so that about ten inches (25 cm) of grass hangs loose. A lemongrass bow hides the bottom wire. Next, glue large, whole bay leaves atop the braid, facing them right and left. After wiring bunches of bay leaves into small fans, glue the fans at angles to the base. Then glue several dried orange and apple slices at various angles, hiding the wires from the bay leaves. Finally, glue pomanders and cinnamon sticks wherever your eye tells you they are needed. ◦

This swag is made with deep green paper ribbon, thyme, garlic bulbs, and cayenne peppers. Cut and unwind three 20-inch (51 cm) lengths of paper ribbon, and braid it together, leaving about 3-1/2 inches (9 cm) at the top for a bow. Wire a paper ribbon bow at the top, and make a hanging loop with the excess wire. Beginning at the bottom of the swag, wire three bunches of dried thyme onto the braid. The blossoms of each group should hide the attachment of the previous one. A fourth bunch is wired facing the opposite direction to overlap the bow. After attaching garlic bulbs at several locations, hot-glue the stems next to each bulb. To fill any holes, and to provide colorful accents, glue red peppers at jaunty angles throughout. Spray this swag with fixative only if you don't plan to use it in your cooking.

Tips for Drying Fruit

While you can easily dry fruit slices by letting them stand at room temperature, undisturbed for several days, the process goes much faster using a dehydrator. This handy device is a bit larger than a bread box, and it has a number of plastic mesh shelves inside. A built-in fan circulates slightly warmed air throughout the chamber, assuring a more even drying of your materials.

Fruit slices can generally be dried using the highest setting. Although you should check the progress periodically, you can expect your materials to be fully dehydrated in about a day and a half.

All fruit will shrink and shrivel a bit during drying, and some will change color. You can prevent apple slices from darkening by dipping them immediately into a mixture of lemon juice and water. To speed the drying process, pat them dry with towels before placing the slices into the dehydrator.

The only "secret" to drying fruit is to make your slices as uniform in thickness as possible. Most often, a 1/8-inch (3 mm) thickness should be sufficient to make a solid slice that won't curl badly.

Although you may be tempted to pluck off an ingredient
here or there, the handsome
appearance of this culinary
wreath will probably stop
your fingers in midmotion.
A lattice of cinnamon sticks
backs a wreath base made of
dried spring onions. Before
adding any other decorations,
turn the onion base face
down, and glue the long cinnamon sticks into a diamond
pattern. Turn the wreath
face up, and glue quince,
pomegranates, poppy pods,
dried orange and apple slices,
pepperberries, rose hips,
and bay leaves into various
locations around the wreath.
For a bit of embellishment,
wire on a dried artichoke. ᵔ

Just for Fun

By now you've probably already concluded that making wreaths, swags, and garlands is anything but a serious business. Here is your chance to stretch your boundaries even further. Try new materials and techniques; dig out those boxes of treasures collected long ago; choose a theme based on a favorite activity. No matter how your experiments turn out—good, bad, or indifferent—you're bound to gain some insight in the process. And who knows? Sometimes the most unlikely combination produces the best results.

A collection of clay pots, a handful of bulbs, and a few hand tools make a decorative statement for the home gardener. Use a wire-reinforced straw base or any other base sturdy enough to support the weight of these materials. Attach the tools first, using a pin made from a length of 18-gauge (heavy) wire. Put hot glue on the ends of the pin, and attach the tools in the bottom center. Hot-glue two sizes of clay pots all around the wreath: about a dozen 2-3/4-inch (7 cm) pots and a half-dozen two-inch (5 cm) pots. Face them all in different directions, adding the smaller ones last. Glue several tulip bulbs into some of the pots and at other likely locations. After cutting one or two lengths of silk blossoms into small pieces, attach picks to the ends, and insert the picks into the wreath. Fill in any open spaces with Spanish moss, using glue or floral pins. Finally, pin loose grapevine to the outside of the wreath to frame the composition. ☙

Another approach to gardening-mania, and the perfect gift for your favorite gardener, is a wreath made totally of useful gardening paraphernalia. Make a base from a 50-foot (15 m) garden hose the same way you would construct a wreath made of vines. Start with a few coils, and spiral the rest of the hose around to secure the circle. Screw a nozzle onto the end of the hose, using it as a decoration. Wire on a second spray nozzle and a couple of hand tools. To attach the clay pot and saucer, drill a tiny hole in one side of the pot and two holes into the saucer. Wire the pot to the saucer, and wire both to the hose. Tuck in a pair of gardening gloves and a few seed packets; then insert Spanish moss into any bare spots. Hot-glue a few dried flower heads onto the moss and, as a last step before delivering your creation, plant a colorful primrose in the clay pot. ☜

124

An Oriental kaleidoscope results from a collection of Polynesian paper fans paired with artificial grape ivy. Start with a straw base wrapped with light brown paper ribbon, and add a wire loop for a hanger. Arrange the fans on both the top and back surfaces of the wreath, using floral pins to secure the fans temporarily. Place the handles facing in on one side, and face them outward on the other. This arrangement produces the kaleidoscope effect. When you are satisfied with their place-ment, hot-glue the fans to the wreath. Finally, use floral pins to attach the silk ivy to the outer rim of the wreath, allow-ing small tendrils to peek out between fans. For extra secu-rity, some ends can be glued between the overlapping edges of the paper ribbon. ☙

As earlier mentioned, literally *anything* can be used as a wreath base. This wreath, built upon a hank of rope, may have been inspired by a late-night western movie. To make it, loop a piece of rope several times, and wire it together at the top around four six-inch (15 cm) wooden picks. The picks provide stability and a firm base for fastening the decorative elements. On the front side, hot-glue several stems of artificial Canadian pine, natural eucalyptus, and a few mahogany pods. Add dried pomegranates, a miniature lotus pod, and a few artificial pears and berries. For a bit of whimsy, glue a mushroom bird (bits of lichen form its wings and tail) to the lowest loop of the rope.

Contributing Designers

Nora Blose and Michelle West
Nora is an herbalist who learned her trade at the knee of her aunt, a country doctor and midwife. Today she has a design studio called Nora's Follies in Candler, North Carolina. Michelle has an in-home boutique in Asheville, North Carolina, where she makes custom arrangements for homes and offices. They often work together on wreaths, swags, and other projects. (Pages 2, 34–35, 37, 38, 46–47, 72, 76, 95, 99, 103, 106)

Julianne Bronder
is a free-lance floral designer, teacher, and display stylist in the Chicago area. She studied at the American Floral Art School in Chicago, and her 15 years of experience as a floral designer also include consulting and floral demonstrations. (Pages 53, 54, 56, 66, 67, 98, 100, 101, 104–105, 109, 122 23, 125)

Janet Frye
owns the Enchanted Florist in Arden, North Carolina, where she enjoys using natural and artificial materials to create dramatic effects with her floral arrangements. A floral designer for 16 years, Janet loves to share her knowledge of flowers, design techniques, and tips for handling wayward materials. (Pages 5, 21, 24, 30, 31, 49 (top), 50–51, 52, 55, 60, 61, 70–71, 80–81, 88 89, 126)

Cynthia Gillooly
owns and operates The Golden Cricket in Asheville, North Carolina. Previously the owner of Weeds 'n' Things in Sanibel Island, Florida, she has applied her unique and artistic vision to floral design for 13 years. Her passion is to use natural materials in somewhat unconventional arrangements. (Pages 26, 33, 49 (bottom), 57, 58, 59, 63, 68, 75, 87, 90, 94, 110–11, 113, 115)

Patti Hill
lives at Mountain Shadows Farm in Weaverville, North Carolina, where she and her husband, John, garden, raise a variety of fowl, and produce honey. In addition to creating wreaths, swags, and garlands, Patti is a weaver, a basket artist, and she makes beaded jewelry. (Pages 27, 39, 40–41, 44, 91, 127)

Christopher Mello
is a horticulturist who comes to floral design through the garden. His first loves are the gardens and woods surrounding his home in Marshall, North Carolina, where he collects many of the materials for his natural arrangements. He practices his art as a floral designer at the Biltmore Estate in Asheville, North Carolina. (Pages 42, 43, 45, 107)

Alyce Nadeau
grows a wide variety of culinary and decorative herbs at her farm, Goldenrod Mountain Herbs, in Deep Gap, North Carolina. Unlike many commercial growers, she plants her herbs in decorative gardens, which are open to the public every August. She markets her herbal creations at trade shows and area farmers' markets. (Pages 36, 78–79, 83, 86, 92–93, 97, 102, 118, 119)

Diane Weaver
and her husband, Dick, own Gourmet Gardens, an herb nursery and craft shop located in Weaverville, North Carolina. Diane takes advantage of her experience as an art director and designer to make wreaths and herbal arrangements using the more than 180 varieties of herbs they grow. (Pages 62, 69, 77, 120–21, 124)

And thanks to . . .
Barbara Applebaum (pages 64–65), Martha Borawa (page 73), Clara Curtis (pages 108, 116–117), Lisa Gibson (pages 112, 128), Jeannette Hafner (pages 85, 96), Anne McCloskey (page 114), Alan Salmon (page 82), Sandy Mush Herb Nursery (pages 28–29, 48), Beth Stickle (pages 6, 74), and Eva Thatcher (page 32).

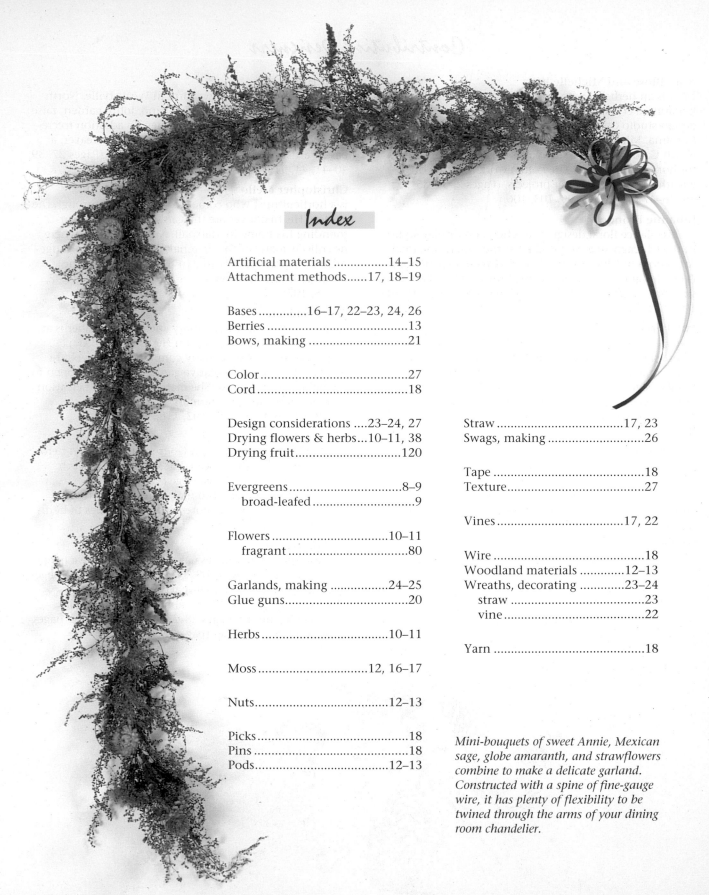

Index

Mini-bouquets of sweet Annie, Mexican sage, globe amaranth, and strawflowers combine to make a delicate garland. Constructed with a spine of fine-gauge wire, it has plenty of flexibility to be twined through the arms of your dining room chandelier.